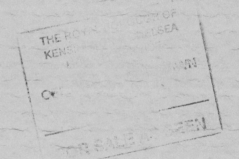

# When I'm Happy...

### Moira Butterfield

WAYLAND

First published in 2014 by Wayland
© Wayland 2014

Wayland
Hachette Children's Books
338 Euston Road
London NW1 3BH

Wayland Australia
Level 17/207 Kent Street
Sydney NSW 2000

Produced for Wayland by
White-Thomson Publishing Ltd
www.wtpub.co.uk
+44 (0) 843 208 7460

Editor: Stephen White-Thomson
Design: Rocket Design (East Anglia) Ltd

A catalogue for this title is available from the British Library

ISBN: 978 0 7502 8281 9
e-book ISBN: 978 0 7502 9125 5

Dewey Number: 152.4'2-dc23

10 9 8 7 6 5 4 3 2 1

Wayland is a division of Hachette Children's Books,
an Hachette UK company.
www.hachette.co.uk

Printed and bound in China

Picture credits:
Dreamstime: Jirasaki 4 and 21, Shutterstock.com: michaeljung 5,
iko 6, Rafael Fernandez Torres 7, Tom Wang 8, Sergey Novikov 9,
lanych 10, Samuel Borges Photography 11, WEExp and Schnapps2012 12,
doglikehorse 13, Ilike 14, Dasha Petrenko 15, Jose Manuel Gelpi Diaz 16,
Tony Moran 18, racom 20, Thinkstock: Wavebreakmedia Ltd 2,
Stockbyte 17, McIninch 19, Daniel Hurst 21.

# When I'm happy, I might...

smile and chuckle...

pull funny faces...

tell silly jokes...

and laugh so much that I wobble like a jelly!

Take a look and see...

Hello. I'm the **Professor of Happiness.**

I'm here to tell you that happiness is good for you!

PROF. HAPPY

When we feel happy, we just can't stop smiling. Check out all our **shiny teeth!**

Bling!

Bling!

There are some great ways to get happy.

You could start by playing your **favourite song.**

La, la! I like this one!

6

# Now find a friend to play a game with.

heave!

**Sooner or later you'll all start laughing.**

## You'll see!

hee, hee!

hee, hee!

**Tell your friends some silly jokes.**

Why do elephants look so wrinkled?

Because they're very hard to iron!

Silly jokes bring **happy smiles.**

Why don't lions eat clowns? Because they taste funny!

Now pull the **funniest face** you can, and get your friends to do the same.

**Playing outside will make you feel happy, especially on a sunny day.**

But even if it rains, you can still splish-splash in the puddles.

**It's fun!**

splish! splash!

15

You could spot some creatures.

# How many can you see?

Put up a tent or build a den.

Then hide inside to have an adventure.

Imagine your tent is a space ship that can...

...zoom you to the stars!

19

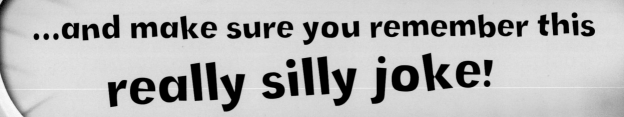

**...and make sure you remember this really silly joke!**

What's invisible and smells of bananas?

Monkey burps, of course!

Lots of love from the Professor of Happiness

PROF. HAPPY

# Do it!

Give your **biggest smile.**

Pull your **funniest face.**

Tell a **silly joke.**

Pretend to **wobble like a jelly.**

PROF. HAPPY

22

Pretend to **splash in a puddle,** just for fun.

Pretend to **zoom in a space rocket.**

Pretend **to tickle someone.**

Pretend you are **being tickled.**

# Teacher's and parent's notes:

These books are designed for children to explore feelings in a fun interactive way. Encourage them to have fun pointing to the pictures, making sounds and doing some acting, too.

During or after your reading, you could encourage your child to talk further about their own feelings, if they want to. Here are some conversation prompts to try:

**Can you think of something that makes you feel happy?**

**What really makes you laugh?**

## Activities to try:

✳ On a piece of paper, draw or paint some funny faces.

✳ On a piece of paper, draw your favourite picture from this book.

## Further reading:

*Your Emotions: I Feel Sad,*
written by Brian Moses and illustrated by Mike Gordon (Wayland)

*Your Emotions: I Feel Angry,*
written by Brian Moses and illustrated by Mike Gordon (Wayland)

*Your Emotions: I Feel Frightened,*
written by Brian Moses and illustrated by Mike Gordon (Wayland)

24